YOUR
CONFIRMATION
in the
CHURCH of ENGLAND

YOUR

CONFIRMATION

in the

CHURCH of ENGLAND

An adult approach to a life
of Christian commitment

STUART THOMAS

First published in 1996 by
KEVIN MAYHEW LTD
Rattlesden
Bury St Edmunds
Suffolk
IP30 0SZ

This book is a reprint of material originally
published by Kevin Mayhew Ltd in 1990 under the title
*Confirmation to Follow: Christian Commitment in the
Church of England*, by Stuart Thomas.

ISBN 0 86209 794 0
Catalogue No. 1500046

Cover illustration: detail of the Britten Window at
Aldeburgh Church, photograph by Derek Forss.
Cover design by Jaquetta Sergeant
Typesetting by Louise Hill
Printed and bound in Great Britain

CONTENTS

Let us run
with perseverance
the race
marked out for us.
(Hebrews 12:1)

INTRODUCTION

You've reached a fairly significant stage in your spiritual life. Perhaps you've reached it because quite recently the Christian faith has started to make sense to you. Probably you want to receive the bread and wine at the Eucharist, and that's a reflection of a deeper longing to know God better. The word Eucharist means 'thanksgiving' in Greek. Your church may call it Holy Communion, Mass or the Lord's Supper, but they all refer to the same service.

You may also be thinking about your place in the Church, or someone else may have convinced you that Confirmation is something you should consider. Whatever the reason, you're reading this book because you're thinking about being confirmed into the Church of England.

Confirmation isn't an end in itself. In a way it's both an end and a beginning – a vital staging post on your spiritual journey. It's important in its own right, but you'll also find resources and guidance to help you on your way afterwards. Later in the book you'll see a description of the Confirmation Service itself, but being confirmed involves much more than a service, and you need more than just a guidebook to tell you about it. What else do you need?

- You need to know what it means to become and to be a Christian – how God has made it possible for you to be forgiven of all that's wrong in your life and live in a loving relationship with him. In particular that means thinking about Baptism, whether or not you've been baptised already. The significance and symbolism of Baptism are an important part of Confirmation, as you'll be remaking your baptismal promises, consciously this time, before the Bishop lays his hands on you.

- Those baptismal promises are the basis of the Christian creed. It's important for you to reflect on what you believe as a Christian. You'll never understand it fully, but that's no reason for not making a start now!

- Confirmation is probably your stepping-stone to receiving the bread and wine at the Eucharist – you may well do so for the first time at your Confirmation service. That's something else you should think over.

- At Confirmation you publicly nail your colours to the mast of the Christian faith. You announce to everyone that you not only believe the Christian creed, but from now on intend to live the Christian life. You need to know what that involves.

- It's vital to begin to understand what the Church is and how you can discover your place in it.

- Reading the Bible and praying are all very well in church – but what about the rest of the time? You'll need some advice on personal prayer and Bible study to help you grow as a Christian.

Maybe that sounds a tall order, but the Christian life has never been a soft option. It's not for those who want to escape from reality for a while, nor for anyone who wants an easy time. It's demanding, but utterly fulfilling – maybe you've already found that out.

This book isn't a complete DIY kit to prepare you for Confirmation. Your local vicar or curate, or trained members of his congregation, will take the main responsibility for that. It's designed to give you a framework for your own understanding of Confirmation and all that it implies. As you read on, questions will occur to you that you'd like answered more fully. Don't hesitate to ask whoever's preparing you – they'll be only too pleased to help.

Chapter One

SQUARE ONE

Becoming a person

Life is a non-stop process of becoming. A baby becomes a toddler; the toddler soon develops into a schoolchild and before long a teenager emerges on the scene.

As an adult, a bachelor may become a husband, a married couple may become parents, then grandparents. We move on from one stage to another in our families, our working lives and in our leisure. Sometimes a family which has had a new arrival will say, 'I wonder what he'll become?' or 'She'll end up just like her mum!' And as junior grows up they watch with interest to see if their predictions come true.

Becoming and being aren't the same thing though. To become a doctor you have to pass certain exams and prove that you've learnt enough during your training to be safe when you're let loose on real patients. Before you can practise as a doctor you need to learn the facts about the human body and the skills to be able to put it right. More than that, you need to acquire the attitudes towards your work and patients that will help you to treat them in the best way possible.

To be a doctor is to put all that into practice, day in, day out, whether or not you feel like it, and regardless of how much some patients annoy you. There are new drugs and medical technology to keep on learning about; mental as well as physical problems to deal with; perhaps hardest of all, coming to terms with people dying.

There's only one 'qualification' for being confirmed – you must have been baptised. That probably happened when you were too young to remember, though it's by no means uncommon for those who are older to be baptised. But whenever you were baptised, you'll be asked by the Bishop at the Confirmation service to repeat your baptismal promises, to affirm what you believe and how you'll live.

It's a public statement that you've become a Christian and intend to be one from this point onwards.

What happens at Baptism

In the New Testament Church anyone who decided to become a 'Follower of the Way' was baptised, usually with the rest of the family. Baptism became the hallmark of Christians and with it they automatically became members of the community of Christians in that place. It meant that they belonged visibly to Christ and therefore also belonged to other followers of Christ. It was a radically new way of life.

The water that's used in baptism is both a 'washing' and a 'drowning'. In the Old Testament there was a ceremony of washing for anyone who wanted to become a member of God's people, the Israelites. It was their way of showing that they'd been cleansed of all the evil practices of their previous religion and culture. John the Baptist took this idea, but preached that even God's people needed to repent of their sin and demonstrate this with a ritual cleansing. After Jesus' death and resurrection, the Early Church saw baptism also as being a sign that the new believer was dying to his old life of sin, and rising to new life in Christ. Paul explains this in his letter to the Romans 6:4: 'We were buried with him through baptism into death in order that . . . we too may live a new life.'

The whole of the Old Testament is based on the promises God made to his people and the promises they made to him in return. It was called 'The Covenant' and was first made by God with Abram; his name became Abraham to make it clear that this experience was to have a permanent effect on his life. The Ten Commandments were part of that Covenant. Sadly, but inevitably, God's people didn't succeed in keeping to their part of the covenant; all too often they went their own way, thinking they knew best, not even learning much from their mistakes. Eventually they ended up being run by other nations and taken into exile in Babylon.

Had God forgotten all his promises to Abraham? The Early Church didn't believe so – they saw Jesus as the fulfilment of all God's promises, and through his death and resurrection all who have faith in him become part of the 'New Covenant'. At the last supper, Jesus said to his disciples as he poured out the wine for them, 'this cup is the new covenant in my blood, which is poured out for you' (Luke 22:20). Baptism therefore means coming under the terms of God's New Covenant.

Jesus once told Nicodemus that 'unless a man is born again he cannot see the Kingdom of God' (John 3:3). Unfortunately the expression 'born again' has become associated with American sects and strange behaviour. Nothing could be further from what Jesus had in mind. He wanted Nicodemus to understand that to follow him was a decisive and final step.

To follow Jesus is to enter into a new life that's as different as life outside the womb is for a new-born baby. That's why in the Baptism service we hear the words: 'Baptism is the sign and seal of this new birth.' It's the sign that the new Christian has been cleaned and washed of all sin and is entering into a totally new life, having 'died' to the old. The seal is the Holy Spirit who comes to fill all Christians and gives them strength and power to live the Christian life. To be baptised is to acknowledge publicly that you're taking that crucial step and allowing God's Holy Spirit to transform and renew your life.

Decision time

In the Baptism service there is a section called 'The Decision'. It consists of three questions, which have to be answered either by the candidate (or if he or she is too young, then by the parents and godparents). These answers show us what's been decided:

1 To turn to Christ

In a nutshell, that's what it is to become a Christian. If someone starts talking to you, your initial reaction is to turn towards them – if you don't, you give them a message that you don't want a conversation with them. Turning to face someone establishes a relationship which can then be continued. We also sometimes say perhaps, that an acquaintance has 'turned to' drink or drugs, because they couldn't find any better way of coping with difficulties. Both those meanings are contained within this answer. We turn to Christ and enter into a relationship with him and we also look to him to give us the power to live every day in his presence.

2 To repent of our sins

When we see God as he really is and recognise Jesus as his Son, who died for our forgiveness and freedom, we begin to understand too that we need to repent – quite literally to 'think again'. No one can claim to be perfect, all of us do and say things which we shouldn't, and we know it. But there's more to repentance than just saying sorry to God in case he gets cross with us. He forgives us through Jesus not just for the specific wrong things we've done, but also for the wrong attitudes and motives which lie behind them – our sinful condition rather than just our specific sins. Repentance isn't like making a New Year's resolution on a permanent basis. It means being honest both with ourselves and with God about the things in our lives which need to be put right; realising that on our own we haven't got a hope of dealing with it; and opening ourselves to receive God's forgiveness, love and power.

3 To renounce evil

When we arrive at a railway station we have to decide which train we're going to take – and that depends on where we've decided to go! To follow Jesus' way is to turn our backs on any other way, because it isn't possible to go in two directions at once. For the first Christians there were plenty of alternative ways, other religions and philosophies they could observe. By comparison the twentieth century may seem a rather irreligious age, but a closer look soon reveals how many choices there are for us. Even people who don't take part in any organised religion put their security in something – ambition, materialism and the pursuit of 'happiness', to name a few. They may appear attractive, but none of these paths leads to God. Jesus said, 'I am the way, the truth and the life. No one comes to the Father except through me.' (John 14:6). One look at a daily newspaper should be enough to convince us that there's a great deal of evil in our world. Governments or other organisations try to eradicate some of it, but selfishness, greed, deceit and exploitation will always be with us. To become a Christian is to turn our backs decisively on the other alternatives the world offers us, reject everything that's opposed to God's ways, and turn firmly towards Christ.

Those three questions come in a particular order. We're drawn to the Christian faith by turning to Jesus and fixing our eyes on him. Only when we've done that will we recognise that we have to repent of all that's wrong in our lives and make a clear decision to turn our backs on evil. Jesus must come first – if he doesn't, we won't see ourselves or our world as they really are. It's turning to him that puts everything else in its true perspective.

When children are baptised, their parents and godparents make the promises on their behalf – older children or adults make them on their own. But in both cases the Church welcomes a new member and promises to play its part in nurturing that person in the Christian faith. Just as we're baptised into the Church, so we're then confirmed into it. Personal faith and commitment are essential but always in the context of the community of Christians.

All of that may sound a bit dry, but the Christian life certainly isn't anything like dry! At the heart of our relationship with God lies an awareness that he loves us. People become Christians for many different reasons, but they'd all agree that their most basic motivation was discovering that God really does love them. No one can 'prove' love in a scientific sense. A baby instinctively recognises its mother's love; a husband and wife don't usually analyse their feelings for one another – they demonstrate their love. At times we make our love for someone conditional. 'I'll love you, provided you . . .' is the message, even if we don't say it quite like that! God loves us without any conditions at all. When we receive his forgiveness and love there are no strings attached, no small print to read first. He isn't a grumpy policeman, noting down our failings in his notebook; nor is he like a strict teacher, finding fault with everything we do. Many years after the events of Jesus' life, which he experienced at first hand, John wrote to one of the early churches, 'This is love, not that we loved God, but that he loved us, and sent his Son as an atoning sacrifice for our sins' (1 John 4:10). God couldn't have done more than that to show how much he loves us. We can't prove his love theoretically, but in responding to it by following Christ, we experience the reality of it for ourselves.

It often happens that people who are baptised as children drift away from the Christian faith as they get older. They never really start to live the christian life for themselves. But then later on they find that they're drawn back to Christianity, whether through a personal crisis, or because a friend has convinced them to give it a try. Confirmation is a great opportunity to remake those baptismal promises personally, but it isn't a second Baptism. Once you've been baptised you've become publicly part of God's family. You can ignore your family, but never leave it! It doesn't make sense to have a second Baptism, but you may feel you'd like to express your new-found faith in Christ and commitment to him. Your local church may be able to help you do this by publicly reaffirming your baptismal promises. Talk about it to your vicar or curate.

Chapter Two

WOULD YOU BELIEVE IT?

Ways of believing

Life involves us in many different kinds of belief. Some are straightforward and we don't even think about them. We believe if we buy a tube of cream cheese that it'll contain what it says on the packet, rather than toothpaste or instant glue! Other beliefs are more complex and often based on our interpretation of events and what we think is likely. What we believe makes a great difference to us. We may believe that driving up the A1 will bring us to Portsmouth, but our mistaken belief won't be much use as we approach the centre of Edinburgh!

What Christians believe

It isn't possible to compare Christian belief directly with an example like that, but throughout its history the Church has sought to establish what is the basis for its beliefs about God, Jesus and the Holy Spirit. In the Baptism service, before the candidates are baptised in water, they (or their parents and godparents) are asked what they believe in a series of three questions. No one needs a theology degree to be a Christian, but a basic understanding of the Christian faith is important, to make sure that our beliefs and faith are properly founded – there's no point believing what isn't right or true.

1 Do you believe in God the Father who made the world?

You don't have to be a Christian to believe in God. It's perfectly possible to accept the existence of a superior being outside our realm of experience, without having to go along with Christianity. It wouldn't be conceivable for a Christian not to believe in God. The question asks more than that, however. It probes into the sort of God we believe in and what his characteristics are.

In the Old Testament God is only rarely described directly as Father, though there are many occasions when his dealings with his people could be called 'fatherly'. (Yes – there are also references to God having motherly qualities.) Throughout his life and ministry Jesus knew God as his heavenly Father – he said, 'The Father is in me and I am in the Father' (John 10:38). Parents should provide guidance and discipline for their families, protect and help them and encourage them to grow up in the right way. They also love them, even when they go wrong.

We wouldn't be alive but for our human parents – we were born because they were there first. In the same way our existence depends on our heavenly Father as Creator, who made everything, ourselves included.

Jesus summed up his Father's love in one of his most famous parables, the Prodigal Son (Luke 15:11-32). When the son asks for his share of the estate, the father lets him have it, even though he knows what might happen. Eventually the son comes to his senses while he's feeding the pigs (the worst job a Jew could possibly have!) and decides to return home and see if he can get work as a servant. He must have wondered how his father would react after the way he'd behaved, but as he approaches the house his father rushes out of the front gate and down the road to kiss and embrace him, dirty and bedraggled though he still is. That night he holds a great party to celebrate the homecoming of his wayward son. That's how God is with us when we return to him. We can only come as we are, spoiled by sin and selfishness and battered by the consequences of our weakness and failures; but he accepts us as we are, forgives us, welcomes us back into his family and gives us everything we need to live in his presence. Sadly, some people have a very poor experience of their father, they've only seen him in a drunken rage, or been neglected and ill-treated. Even so, they've got some idea of what a father should be like – and God, our heavenly Father, goes beyond that in every way!

If we stand on the Alps or the Himalayas, overwhelmed

by the grandeur of the mountain scenery; or watch the sea pounding against the shoreline on a stormy day, we feel pretty small and helpless in comparison. One person pitted against the forces of nature seems like very unfair competition! The earth is 25,000 miles around the Equator and varies from 29,000 feet above sea level at the top of Everest to 36,000 feet under water in the Challenger Deep. The centre of the earth is about 4,000 miles from its surface. The moon is 238,000 miles away, the sun 93 million miles; and then we realise that earth, our home, is a tiny dot in the Milky Way galaxy. Our sun is just one medium sized star among 18,000 million others in it and the Milky Way is just one galaxy of stars! The beauty and wonder of our own planet, the immensity beyond imagination of the Universe, and the orderliness of the whole of Creation, point us to the One who brought it into being.

If we study a painting in a gallery we may be able to identify the artist; when we hear a piece of music we may be able to recognise the composer. An artist's character, a composer's emotions are reflected in the work of art he creates, similarly with our Creator God. In what he's made we see his goodness and love, his beauty and majesty, and yet this mighty Creator who made the whole Universe and is sovereign over it, wants us, his creatures, to know him as intimately as we know our parents. He's no remote Designer, leaving the world he's made to run on like a 'clockwork orange'. On the contrary, he's intimately involved with his creation. Jesus taught us to talk to God as 'Our Father in Heaven' (Matthew 6:9). Just as he knew his heavenly Father and trusted him totally, so he wants us to share in that relationship; to know that God is our Father and we're his children; to enjoy his presence throughout our lives and his strength to help us live his way.

2 *Do you believe and trust in his Son Jesus Christ, who redeemed mankind?*

It's not too hard to believe in some sort of god, one who had something to do with creating the world, but remains impersonal and distant. On the whole that kind of god is easy enough to get along with. He may not get too involved with our lives, but he doesn't get in our way either. Christianity has never believed in a god like that. At the heart of the Christian faith is Jesus Christ – in fact it couldn't be the Christian faith without him! By any standards, Jesus cuts an extraordinary figure. No human being has had a more profound effect on the world and yet he was born into an ordinary home and received no special education. He never travelled beyond his native Palestine and never published any of his thoughts or philosophy. He didn't hold any government or church office and didn't mix with important people.

Quite the opposite – he made himself extremely unpopular by speaking out against the hypocrisy and self-righteousness of the religious leaders of his day. Instead of mixing with the upper crust and the people of influence, Jesus spent much of his time with ordinary folk and society's cast-offs. He was arrested for no good reason, was condemned at a blatantly unfair trial, and in the end was killed as a criminal on a Roman gibbet, that had been set up on a hill outside Jerusalem which served as the corporation rubbish tip. It was a cruel and barbaric death.

Why do Christians focus so much of their attention on this remarkable individual? The Gospels record one of the great teachers of all time – no one ever gave more profound insights into our human condition and God's purposes. The Sermon on the Mount has been regarded by many people as one of the most memorable pieces of teaching ever given, though its standards seem almost unattainable, so high are they. Jesus' teaching was reinforced by his actions – he went about healing the sick and handicapped, restoring them to a whole new way of life; he miraculously provided a meal for 5,000 people from one small boy's rather squashed picnic lunch. His love and compassion, his integrity and single-mindedness are an example to us all, though we recognise Jesus as someone quite unique. But special as these things are, they don't on their own support the reason why Jesus is the central point of the Christian faith, although they undoubtedly draw us towards that conclusion.

Our lives are deeply scarred with the effects of sin, whether it's our own or other people's, however successful and happy we may appear on the surface. We try to go it alone and manage without God, only to fall flat on our faces. There's nothing we can do to extricate ourselves from the mess we get ourselves into. So God came to the rescue, knowing that it was the only way to bring us back into a relationship with himself – 'God so loved the world that he gave his one and only Son, that whoever believes in him should not perish but have eternal life' (John 3:16). Jesus' Cross is the focal point of the Christian faith – the key event in the history of God's dealings with mankind. He suffered and died to defeat all the forces of evil and death and to win for us forgiveness and freedom. His death releases us from the paralysing grip of sin, guilt and death to enjoy a completely new life in God's loving presence. Our sins were like a barrier separating us from God, just as the Berlin Wall separated two halves of a city. That's now been demolished once and for all. In the same way Jesus' death and resurrection have smashed down what Paul calls 'the dividing wall of hostility' between us and God (Ephesians 2:15). There's no longer anything to separate us from God's love.

A new baby's arrival often provokes comments like 'Oh, she's the image of her mum!' or 'Jimmy's got a temper just like his dad's!' Children usually reflect something of their parents. In Jesus, we see something of what our heavenly Father is like – he came to show us God in a way we could understand. He shared our human life in every way, experienced all the things we're familiar with and knew what it was to be human. If his life had ended with his crucifixion, we'd be left with the story of a great teacher and remarkable man who came to a tragic and undeserved end. But Jesus' death was the final part of God's plan – without it sin and death would have remained not dealt with. The writers of the New Testament saw clearly how God had been working throughout the history of his people towards the day when he would finally bring to fulfilment in Jesus all his purposes. Jesus' death wasn't the end. No film-director could ever have dreamed up a finale like the resurrection, but it wasn't a finale at all. God didn't want to create the ultimate happy ending. The resurrection is the final chapter in the story of our salvation – without it there wouldn't be a Christian faith. Through it we can revel in the new resurrection life which we share with Jesus, through faith in him. As the hymn-writer puts it, 'Ransomed, healed, restored, forgiven, who like thee his praise should sing?'

In the Baptism service, the priest asks God to bless the water with the words, 'Bless this water, so that . . . who is washed in it may be made one with Christ in his death and resurrection, to be cleansed and delivered from all sin.' Jesus Christ is at the very heart of the Christian faith. Only in him can we receive forgiveness and experience new life.

3 Do you believe and trust in the Holy Spirit, who gives life to the people of God?

The evidence of the world around us makes belief in some sort of God a reasonable option. There's enough historical data to demonstrate the existence of the man Jesus and, on that basis, many have accepted him as God's Son. The Father and the Son are straightforward enough, but what about the Holy Spirit? Christians believe that God is three persons in one God, the Holy Trinity. The Holy Spirit is the third person, every bit as much part of God as Jesus and as real and personal as the Father and the Son. He was present at the creation of the world (Genesis 1:2) and appears throughout the Old Testament. The prophet Joel clearly foresaw the day when God 'will pour out his Spirit on everyone' (Joel 2:28). Jesus was conceived by the power of the Holy Spirit and at his baptism that same Spirit came upon him to give him the power for his ministry. It was God's Spirit who raised Jesus from the dead.

Jesus warned the disciples that he wouldn't be with them

forever, but he promised that the Holy Spirit would come upon them to enable them to continue where he'd left off – he'd done the work his Father had given him and now his followers would carry on proclaiming the good news of God's Kingdom. So when the day of Pentecost came, Peter and the other disciples experienced the outpouring of the Holy Spirit so dramatically, they realised that Joel's prophecy was being fulfilled in and through them. It's no surprise that they preached the need for repentance and baptism for the forgiveness of sins, followed by the gift of the Holy Spirit (Acts 2:38). Both were equally important. As the new Christians were baptised they received the Holy Spirit, and ever since then, Christians have regarded Baptism as the time when he comes upon them as the presence of God in their lives. There may be a delay between an adult making a positive commitment of his life to Jesus Christ and being baptised.

Not everyone makes this sort of commitment in one clear moment and all of us have to recommit ourselves to him throughout our Christian lives. At Confirmation the Holy Spirit comes on the candidates to give them the strength they need to live the Christian life. As the bishop lays hands on them he asks God to confirm them with his Holy Spirit. It's the end of the process of commitment, but the beginning of a totally transformed life. He shows us Jesus and reveals to us how much we need him. He plants the seed of faith in us and enables our faith to flourish and grow. He gives us gifts so that we can serve God and live as he wants us to and strength to face the obstacles and trials of this world. He fills us with joy and love, transforming our relationships and the way we see things. We can't see him, but like the wind we know he's there by the effect he has on our lives and other people's too.

Before he lays his hands on you to pray for you to receive the Spirit, the Bishop says a very ancient prayer based on Isaiah 11, in which he asks that those to be confirmed will be filled with God's Spirit and demonstrate this in their lives. Why not read it now (you'll find it printed in the section of this book about the Confirmation service) and pray it yourself as part of your personal preparation?

It's one thing to believe a theory or fact. We believe Australia exists, but unless we visit or have any connections with the place, it remains an academic fact. To believe *in* something is altogether different, because it implies that it makes a difference to our lives. The questions in the Baptism service don't ask if we believe there is a God, but whether or not we believe and trust in him. The Christian faith remains just one creed or philosophy among many unless we accept it's true for us and live accordingly.

At Confirmation we acknowledge that we believe in one God, the Father, the Son and the Holy Spirit. On a much deeper level we announce to everyone present that we know God the Creator as our loving heavenly Father, through his Son Jesus Christ, by the power of his Holy Spirit.

Chapter Three

PERSONAL BELONGING

We all need to know that we belong to someone or something. One of the first things a baby learns is who it belongs to – childcare experts call it 'bonding'. A child who grows up, not knowing where it belongs or who it belongs to, will become a sad and confused adult. Belonging usually has a symbol of some sort. Children sometimes pin badges to their clothes, while adults may put a sticker in the car window. School uniform helps create a sense of community, while sports teams wear particular colours not just to be identified easily – it reinforces that this is a team. Old Boy ties, college scarves, club badges, town coats-of-arms, national flags – all of them emphasise who and what we're part of. On a more personal level a married couple will wear rings to symbolise their love for each other and that they belong together – often they'll carry a photograph around with them too.

The Eucharist is also a symbol of belonging. Whenever we receive the bread and wine we're reminded that we belong to Jesus and to God's Kingdom; that we're part of the community of Christians called the Church. The most immediate difference that confirmation will have on you is that you'll be able to receive the bread and wine.

In the early years of the church, children probably did so from the time they were baptised (this is still the practice in the Orthodox Church), but since the Reformation, the Church of England, like the other 'reformed' churches, has delayed the time of admission to Communion until the child has reached 'the years of discretion' – until it has a reasonably adult understanding of the Christian faith, traditionally in the teenage years. Although a growing number of churches now admit people to Communion before they're confirmed, the rule is still, broadly speaking, that you shouldn't receive the bread and wine until after Confirmation. Many Confirmation services now include a Eucharist so that the newly-confirmed can take Communion for the first time.

Like Baptism, the Eucharist is a sacrament – what the 1662 Prayer Book calls 'an outward sign of an inward grace'. In other words, it's more than just a simple reminder in case we'd forgotten. It makes real to us in a visible way what God has been doing in the deepest parts of our lives, transforming us and giving us all we need to live in a way which pleases him.

On the night of his arrest and trial, Jesus shared the Passover meal with his disciples. When it came to the breaking of the unleavened bread, he broke it with these words: 'This is my body, given for you. Do this in remembrance of me.' Later, when the meal was over, he shared the cup of wine with them: 'This cup is the New Covenant in my blood, which is poured out for you' (Luke 22:19-20).

Although the earliest Christians continued to worship in the Temple and synagogues, they also met in each other's homes for a fellowship meal. During this they would obey Jesus' command and share the bread and wine as an act of worship and remembrance (Acts 2:42). Because they referred to it as Jesus' body and blood, the early Christians were accused in some places of cannibalism! They didn't always behave too well either. Paul had to remind the Christians at Corinth to treat the Lord's Supper properly and reverently, so that they didn't 'eat the bread or drink the cup of the Lord in an unworthy manner' (1 Corinthians 11:27). This passage written by Paul has been used as the basis for the wording of the 'thanksgiving' prayer by churches ever since, to remember Jesus' death and resurrection until he returns in glory. The celebration of the Eucharist has been one of the central parts of the church's worship throughout its history, all over the world. In the Alternative Service Book the Eucharistic Prayer ('Eucharist' is a Greek word meaning 'thanksgiving') incorporates an acclamation said by the whole congregation:

Christ has died.
Christ is risen.
Christ will come again.

It isn't there just to remind us of certain historical facts – we must never forget their importance for us.

We come to God with our praise

One of the first events in a typical service is that a hymn will be sung by everyone present. This is very often a great hymn of praise to God and it helps us to focus on him before anything else. If we fail to do this, we think of ourselves and our own concerns, and immediately put everything out of perspective. We come to worship and bring our praises to God for all that he is and all that he's done. Everything else that happens in the service has to be in context of giving glory to God.

We come to God with our sins and weakness

Whatever the language and style of the service, each Eucharist includes the Confession and Absolution. Before we can receive the bread and wine worthily, we come to God to acknowledge our sin. We aren't doing God a favour by coming to meet him – like the Prodigal Son we don't really deserve to come into his presence at all. In the Prayer of Humble Access, often used at Communion, we say together: 'We are not worthy so much as to gather up the crumbs under your table.' It isn't grovelling humility, but an honest recognition that our selfish attitudes, deceitful words and hurtful actions have spoiled our relationship with God and other people and damaged our lives. We don't come to God as an exercise of our rights, but depending totally on his love and mercy. Our repentance is much more than just regret at being found out – it's a determined commitment to live in the power of the Holy Spirit as God wants us to. It's also based on our conviction that God will keep his promise to forgive and restore us.

Sometimes our attitudes are so entrenched that we remain quite oblivious of our need of forgiveness – it never occurs to us that we're in the wrong! The Confession we say together asks God to forgive us even for our unrecognised sins – the things we've ignored, forgotten about or pretended are nothing to do with us. Nothing is beyond the reach of God's love and forgiveness. The writer of the letter to the Hebrews says, 'He is able to save completely those who come to God through him' (Hebrews 7:25). That doesn't mean we can go away and do what we like afterwards. In the Absolution, the President (the priest responsible for saying the thanksgiving prayer) assures us of God's forgiveness and asks that God will 'confirm and strengthen us in all goodness'. Only God's Spirit living within us helps us not to fall back into our old ways. Inevitably we fail – far more often than we want to – but God will always receive us when we turn back to him and help us to live the new life which is ours in Christ.

Jesus once told a parable about a man who was let off a huge debt, only to refuse forgiveness to someone else who owed him a very small amount. The Peace, which comes just before the Eucharistic Prayer in the Alternative Service Book, is more than a quick break, or a chance to greet our fellow worshippers, it's an opportunity to put right any relationships that have gone wrong between ourselves and anyone else. We all come to God as forgiven sinners and we must be willing to forgive others too.

When we come into God's presence we can't pretend to be what we're not. Others may see a 'plastic' smile and not recognise the anxiety or anger that lies behind it – we all have times when our faces don't match up to our feelings. God knows us through and through – the Psalmist says, 'O Lord you have searched me and you know me. You know when I sit and when I rise: you perceive my thoughts from afar.' (Psalm 139:1-2). God knows us better even than we know ourselves. He's well aware of all the weakness and fear and sinfulness. But he still wants us to come to his Table, to share his heavenly banquet. As we leave our seats to come to the altar rail we're reminded that we come as we are, feelings and all. We can be sure that's how God accepts us.

We come to God with our gifts

Worshipping God doesn't involve switching off the rest of our lives – we couldn't even if we wanted to. Our whole lives are part of our worship: our hopes and fears, our work and leisure, our joy and sadness. The bread and wine and the money we give sum up all that we have and are. Our work and skill, our energy and commitment are all contained in what we give. We may think we're amazingly generous, but everything we have is given us on trust by God – including our time, our abilities and our energy. The Offertory Prayer highlights this, using the words of David from 1 Chronicles 29:14: 'Yours, Lord, is the greatness, the power, the glory, the splendour and the majesty, for everything in heaven and on earth is yours. All things come from you and of your own do we give you.' God owes us nothing, yet gives us everything. What we offer back to him is a symbol of our love for him and our commitment to him. Giving of ourselves is something we can do gladly and willingly, for as Paul puts it, 'God loves a cheerful giver' (2 Corinthians 9:7).

The bread and wine symbolise more than our work though. They're made by crushing corn and grapes. The original produce has to be 'destroyed' to make the bread and wine. That's a picture of the dying and rising again which are the heart of our faith. For as Jesus died and was raised to new life, so do we in him. Our old life of sin has gone – we're dead to it, but alive to God in Jesus Christ.

We come to God with our thanks

The Thanksgiving Prayer is said by the President on behalf of everyone present, although in the Alternative Service Book there are points at which the congregation joins in with the words. After it the bread and wine are normally regarded as *consecrated*, or set apart exclusively for use in worship. They're still bread and wine, but because of what they represent, great care is taken to ensure they're treated reverently. The first part of the prayer is sometimes called the Preface, because it comes before the 'Institution Narrative' – in it we thank and praise God for creating us and bringing us into a new living relationship with himself through his Son Jesus Christ. He is worthy of all our praise and worship because he is our heavenly Father. The word 'worship' comes from the Old English word *'worthscip'*. We're giving God, quite literally, the praise and worship which are his by right. His Son, Jesus, was born a human being, in every respect like us. He lived an ordinary yet extraordinary life, was killed on a criminal's cross and raised to new life – so that we could be forgiven and free! Through his resurrection, sin and death are defeated for ever and he now reigns in glory with his Father. He sends the Holy Spirit on us to assure us that we belong to God. So, at the end of this section, the whole congregation joins in the words of the Sanctus: 'Holy, holy holy Lord, God of power and might. Heaven and earth are full of your glory. Hosanna in the highest!'

After this crescendo of praise, the President asks the Holy Spirit to make the bread and wine real to us as the body and blood of our Lord Jesus, and then continues with the 'Institution Narrative', which reminds us of Jesus' words to his disciples at the Last Supper, when he broke the bread and shared the cup of wine with them. Our forgiveness and new life depend directly on Jesus' suffering and dying for us. After this the congregation affirm together that Christ has died (it's already happened), Christ is risen (it's a present reality), Christ will come again (it's our hope for the future).

The final part of the prayer sums up the Eucharist. In it we remember Jesus' death for us on the Cross and announce to everyone the truth of his resurrection and ascension. Until he comes in glory, we'll continue to celebrate his one perfect sacrifice by regularly receiving the bread and wine. We ask God to accept our gifts and thanks and worship and fill us with his love and his Spirit. Receiving Communion isn't a weekly 'fix' to keep us going till the next time, but should make a real difference to our lives every day, not just to our relationship with God, but to the contacts we have with other people as well. The whole prayer ends with a great acclamation of praise, which brings our attention wholly back to God and his Son Jesus Christ. We can never thank him enough for all he's done for us, and continues to do, but we can show our gratitude by the way we live every day.

We come to God with our prayers

It would be wrong to allow our worship to become an exclusive personal relationship between God and us. God's love in our hearts means we'll have a genuine concern for the world around us, for those we know who are suffering, for our country or home area, or even for events in other parts of the world. In every service there's an opportunity to bring these concerns to God in prayer, incorporate them in our worship, and allow God to speak to us too. Unless we've been asked to lead the prayers, it may be that what we'd like to say remains unspoken, but we can bring it to God in the silence of our hearts.

We come to God with our commitment

Receiving the bread and wine isn't a weekly 'treatment' for our souls, that makes us feel better and helps us cope with life. The first half of the Eucharist is called the 'Ministry of the Word', the central point of which is the reading and explanation of God's Word. The sermon encourages us to learn more about God and his ways, to meditate on part of the Bible, and to think about how that should affect us day by day. Worship doesn't mean we can put our minds into neutral gear! Our wills must also be influenced. Just before the end of the service, the congregation joins together in praying:

> Send us out in the power of your Spirit
> to live and work to your praise and glory.

We need the Holy Spirit each day to give us the strength and will to serve God as well as possible, not just in our church fellowship, but equally in our families, our workplaces, among our friends, or in wider society. That may involve something as unglamorous as flower-arranging, as energy-sapping as teaching in the Junior Church, or as influential as being engaged in local politics. None of this will earn us God's favour or love – he gives us that anyway. Forgiveness, freedom, a new life – all are ours absolutely free. We couldn't earn them if we tried. Out of his grace God restores us to being his children again. We serve him wherever he calls us, not from duty, but as an expression of our love for him and because we want to share his love with others. We'll fail often, because we think we can go it alone, but when we allow the Holy Spirit to live in us and give us his power, we'll find the strength to do what God calls us to do.

As you come for the first time to receive the bread and wine, allow the words and actions of the service to speak to you. Be open to God's love and strengthened by his Spirit.

Confirmation isn't part of an obstacle course you have to complete before you can take Communion, but you'll find that as you remake your baptismal promises and learn more of the Christian faith during your preparation for being confirmed, you'll come to a greater understanding of all that God has done for you in Jesus Christ. A lifetime isn't enough to take this in fully, but as you continue to receive the bread and wine on a regular basis, not only will you realise more, but you'll also find your love for God deepening and maturing.

A typical Eucharist

Preparation

A Hymn is sung, usually full of praise and glory to God, during which the ministers and choir may enter and take their places, if they haven't already.

The Welcome is said by the President (who will later preside at the Eucharist itself).

The Collect for Purity is said by everyone; it's a very ancient prayer, asking God to make us clean and fit to enter his presence.

The Confession and Absolution come either now, or after the Intercessions.

The Gloria is said or sung at this point.

The Collect, or special prayer for the day, is said by the President.

Ministry of the Word

The Old and/or New Testament Readings come next, usually read by a member of the congregation. A hymn or psalm may follow them.

The Gospel Reading is announced and read out, with the congregation standing. Its importance is emphasised by the responses before and after it's read out.

The Sermon is given, often explaining what's been read out, or sometimes addressing an important issue or theme.

The Creed, the basis of what Christians believe, is said by everyone.

The Intercessions, or prayers, follow, usually led by a member of the congregation. They'll cover the needs of the Church, the world, and any particular local needs or problems, as well as those who are suffering.

The Prayer of Humble Access may now be said by the whole congregation, unless the Confession and Absolution have not been said earlier.

Ministry of the Sacrament

The Peace leads from the Ministry of the Word (all that's happened up till now) into the Ministry of the Sacrament. It's usual for worshippers to share the Peace with each other. A hymn often follows, during which the gifts may be brought to the Holy Table, so that it can be prepared. When all is ready, everyone joins in the words of the **Offertory Prayer**.

The Eucharist Prayer is now said by the President – the congregational responses may be either said or sung.

The Lord's Prayer will also be said or sung by all, immediately after the prayer has finished. The President then **Breaks the Bread** which is shared by everyone and **Invites** them to come and receive the bread and wine.

After Communion

After Communion has been distributed to everyone, a **Final Prayer** is said together before the President **Blesses** and **Dismisses** the congregation. A final **Hymn** is normally sung to end the service.

Based on the Alternative Service Book – Rite 'A'

Chapter Four

ACTIVE SERVICE

We've already seen how important it is for people to belong. One of the results of that is the number of clubs and societies which they set up and join. If there's a common interest, people will club together to pursue it. Cricket or computers, music or marmalade-making, keeping fit or keeping rabbits – you can be sure there's an organisation just for that! Frequently there's some visible evidence of club membership.

Members are usually expected to take part in the activities of the organisation they belong to and support its aims and goals with their energy and money. The Church isn't a club or society in the usually accepted sense. A former Archbishop of Canterbury once stated that the Church is 'the only organisation which exists purely for the benefit of non-members'. On the surface it isn't a huge one. Only about 8 per cent of the population go to church at all and of those only a minority attend their local parish church. Although these figures apply to the United Kingdom, they're reflected throughout much of the Western World.

Many people still prefer a church wedding or funeral, but show great reluctance to worship in church on a more regular basis, except perhaps for Christmas or Easter.

This book is about being confirmed into the Church of England, although some of its contents could be applied to any Christian church. When you're confirmed, it doesn't mean you're being initiated into an exclusive club which has a select membership list, nor is it just about being admitted to Communion, though that's certainly important. Once you've been confirmed, you become an active adult member of God's Church, that extraordinary, infuriating and lovable organisation whose reason for existing lies entirely in those who aren't part of it and probably would prefer to stay that way! Regrettably, there are churches which do resemble a closed society. They give the impression that unless you've reached a certain social and educational level or don't mind spending all your spare time in a frenzy of meetings and a welter of activity, you can't become an accepted member. Christian commitment doesn't involve the whole church rushing round in ever-decreasing circles and sucking anyone in range into an organisational vortex. There has to be time for relaxation, for meditation and reflection, if there's to be any real spiritual growth. On the other hand confirmed members of the Church can hardly claim that its activities don't concern them.

In Acts 2 we have a picture of how the Church was organised in its earliest days. Life is rather different now and we can't expect to copy it in every detail, but we can draw from it a framework or pattern for church organisation and involvement to help us understand how we might fit in and what part we should be playing.

Discipleship

The first disciples were called by Jesus to follow him and share in his ministry. They spent nearly three years with him, listening to his teaching, watching all that he did, seeing at first hand God's plans coming to their ultimate fulfilment. Ordinary folk they may have been but, because of their experience, there was nobody in the community of believers which worshipped Jesus who had more authority or knowledge – they'd been the ones closest to the Lord. But their authority was based not only on their knowledge and personal relationship with Jesus, it was founded at least as much on their experience of the Holy Spirit at Pentecost. Just as the Spirit had come upon Jesus at his baptism to empower him for his ministry and confirm his unique status as God's Son, so he also came upon the disciples to give them power and strength and to give their teaching and ministry the authority of God himself. It followed that as they themselves taught the new believers, they emphasised that all who follow the Lord Jesus will be filled with the Holy Spirit too, to assure them that they are God's children, loved by him and to give them the resources they need to serve him. The whole of the early Church lived according to this principle. In his various letters to the earliest churches, Paul seems to take it as read that being filled with the Holy Spirit will be a central part of every Christian's experience. In 1 Corinthians 12 he lists some of the gifts of the Holy Spirit, which all Christians receive to enable them to play their part in the ministry of the whole Church and to serve him in the world. It's when we use these ministries and gifts that we're being disciples, living in the power of the Spirit; we're also doing it, not for self-indulgence, but for the 'common good of humanity'.

Discipleship means 'following' – following Jesus not merely as a good example, but more as a pattern for our ministry. Ministry isn't restricted to those who are ordained or who seem to be especially holy; every believer has to play his part. Gifts such as prophecy, discernment, faith and healing are all just as necessary in the twentieth century as they were in the first, even if they're exercised in slightly different ways. They help God's people to grow in worship and love and fellowship and form the basis of the Church's witness to the world around.

For example, many churches today are discovering the ministry of Christian healing, not just as a quick alternative to the health service, but fundamentally as a way of bringing God's wholeness to others as Jesus did – a healing which goes far deeper than bodily disorders, to the parts no medicine or treatment can reach. Not everyone is given a specific ministry of healing, but every Church member is involved in supporting those who do and in bringing God's wholeness to the situations in which they're put. To use Paul's picture, we're all different parts of a body, each fulfilling our own function as a contribution to the life, health and activity of the whole of that body.

Disciples are learners before they're doers, however. Discipleship requires us to be quiet and attentive listeners as well. The early Christians sat and listened to the apostles' teaching before anything else, just as the disciples them-selves had learned from their Master. It's all too easy to get trapped in a maelstrom of doing things (all of which may be very good in themselves) and to end up in a spiritual rut, because we haven't taken time to listen and learn.

Evangelism, healing, service in the world – all these are vital, but they'll never be effective unless they're exercised by disciples who've been filled with the Holy Spirit and are always open to learn from him and receive his gifts. This is the heart of Confirmation, as you'll realise again when you look back to the prayer the Bishop says before he lays hands on those who are to be confirmed. Read it again now and pray it for yourself, or for anyone else you know who's being confirmed.

Worship

The early Christians were really keen! Every day, on their way to prayers in the Temple, they would meet together and pray in the outer courtyards. They also met regularly for a 'fellowship meal' during which they would obey Jesus' command and break bread together to remember his death and resurrection until his coming again in glory, which they expected at any time. They were noted for praising God, as the jailer and other prisoners at Philippi discovered when Paul and Silas were imprisoned there. Almost two thousand years have passed since then and the Church looks very different. It's adapted to cultures and conditions right across the world; it's adopted all manner of structures of authority; it's created various traditions throughout its history of music, art, literature, social activity and so on. But wherever it's found itself, at whatever point in time, the Church has always worshipped the same God as its central activity.

Worship is the highest and greatest activity we can ever take part in. We are literally giving God his worth. As we worship God we become more fully human, more as God created us to be.

The Church at worship is much more than the sum total of its parts though. We all bring our individual praise and thanksgiving but as we celebrate together God's love and mercy, his grace and forgiveness, we find that we're caught up in something far greater than we could know on our own. Although the New Testament stresses the importance of a personal relationship with God through Christ, it also sets an equal priority on our corporate life as Christians. Nowhere does the word 'saint' appear in the singular, except in the expression 'let every saint'. We can't live in a spiritual 'bubble' of our own, isolated from other Christians, doing our own thing with God. We're all forgiven and restored sinners. We're all children of God, members of his family. That's how we must live and worship.

Since worship comes from our hearts it follows that it will be to some extent emotional. Some worshippers try to remove all traces of emotion from worship, but that is neither helpful, nor possible. Extreme emotionalism that loses its grip on reality is dangerous; but cold, academic, or insensitive worship is hardly more desirable. Everyone will have different ways of expressing their emotions, but there's nothing wrong with being enthused and excited by our experience of God, through Jesus Christ, in the power of his Holy Spirit. It's a foretaste of Heaven where, as Charles Wesley put it, we'll be 'lost in wonder, love and praise'.

Fellowship

As Christians we belong first and foremost to God, but because of that we also belong to one another. One of the most striking things about the Early Church was the way in which everyone came together and shared what they had with each other. Nobody was allowed to remain in need, because those who had enough money and possessions were only too willing to give of what they had, to provide for those who had little. They cared about and for each other, enjoyed meeting together and sharing their new faith. A cricket team is not simply made up of eleven talented individuals. The team isn't likely to win any trophies if the members are more concerned with showing off their own abilities than working as a cohesive unit. Successful teams are those which learn to pull together, recognise and play to each other's strengths and abilities and help each other out. Even in the earliest days of the Church there were disputes and conflicts – Paul was well aware of them, as we can see from many of his letters. Despite this, Christians are still called to love one another. Jesus once said to his disciples: 'All men will know that you are my disciples if you love one another' (John 13:35). His command to love one another is equally binding on us. The world's standard is usually to put its own interest on the top of the pile. 'You've got the right to decide how to live your life!' scream the popular media; 'Do what's in your best interests'. We don't need to neglect ourselves in a stupid or attention-seeking way, but we should recognise that our own self-interest can often cause other people suffering or misery. Our fellowship must display to the rest of the world the standards of Jesus and the effect his love has on our relationships.

Stewardship

C. S. Lewis once said that Christian giving only starts when it hurts us! Most of us are willing to put something in the collection plate or the Christian Aid envelope. The Early Church went well beyond that – they were willing to sell their possessions so that they could give to those whose need was greater than their own. There was no distinction between the haves and the have-nots. It probably didn't stay that way for long. By the time James wrote his letter, it appears that there were seats for the well-off, but standing room only for the poor (James 2:1-4). We've no right to flaunt our wealth and assume it entitles us to greater status, because everything we have comes from God. He gives it to us on trust, to use in his service, not to buy ourselves privilege or indulge ourselves at the expense of others. Someone once pointed out that the last part of us to be converted is our wallet! When we give money to God's work, we're not giving just to the Church or some other institution – above all we're giving it back to God. Our money is part of us – it sums us up. It reflects the time and energy and commitment we've given up to acquire it, and in our society, it also reflects status and skill. Nevertheless, we have to bear in mind that our employment, skills and energy are also gifts from God.

The Old Testament tells us about the tithe. Everyone in the community gave a tenth of all they had back to God. It was used not just for temple maintenance, but for the benefit of the whole community, especially the poor and those who were less able to look after themselves. Although the New Testament fixes no specific amount that Christians should give, many still try to keep to that 10 per cent guideline. There's more to stewardship than writing an occasional cheque or taking out some of our savings – not everyone can afford to do that, but all Christians can contribute their time and abilities to God's Kingdom, whether that's in the Church or some other organisation.

God has given us everything we have – his generosity to us is limitless. We, in turn, can give as generously as possible of what we can offer; nothing's so small that God can't use it. God isn't after those who can give the most; as Paul told the Corinthians, 'The Lord loves a cheerful giver' (2 Corinthians 8:7).

Leadership

Sports teams have captains; companies have directors and chairmen; countries have kings or presidents. Leaders are necessary for any group of people to work well together, however large or small. We often think of the leaders of the Church in terms of bishops and archbishops, who come to mind dressed up in copes and mitres looking like a production of the Mikado! In fact, many of their duties don't require them to dress up. Their work covers a huge area of responsibility, as well as a large geographical area. That's why each parish has a leader too, called a vicar or rector. He may well have a curate or deacon working for him, if the parish is a large one. Leaders have an image of being terribly dictatorial and authoritarian and it wouldn't be fair to deny that Church leaders have also fallen into this trap at times. But the Christian standard of leadership is quite clear – all authority comes from God and those who exercise it do so under his control. Jesus made it clear right through his ministry that he spoke and acted only on his Father's authority, although many who heard him said, 'He speaks as one who has authority.' His followers recognised this, and were amazed that he should see fit to kneel down and wash their feet. Only the most menial servants did such tasks. Christian leaders aren't there to call all the shots or dictate terms to everyone, but to act as servants. That doesn't preclude them from taking responsibility or making decisions, but it shows them how to go about it.

One day Jesus' disciples were squabbling about their status. He responded by saying, 'You know that those who are regarded as rulers of the Gentiles lord it over them, and their high officials exercise authority over them. Not so with you. Instead, whoever wants to become great among you must be your servant, and whoever wants to be first must be the willing slave of all. For the Son of Man did not come to be served but to serve, and to give his life as a ransom for many.' (Mark 10:42-45).

In a sense all Christians are called to share in leadership, though mostly that's focused on one or two individuals. Part of that sharing involves respecting those who have authority in our church, not least those at the top, whom we love to criticise! Church leaders take a lot of criticism, and while this may be justified at times (they're only human!), their work is often sensitive and demanding and they need our prayers and support too. If it isn't possible to share their responsibilities, we can help in sharing their burden.

Two of Paul's longest letters are to the church at Corinth. It was a church with great gifts and many resources, but it came adrift because of internal strife – individuals were using the gifts of the Holy Spirit to promote themselves and show off, with the inevitable result that disputes and rows erupted. Paul's teaching to them and to us, is that these gifts are for the good of all, to be used in serving others. We can all discover and use our own gifts to minister in some capacity for the glory of God and the development of his Church. There's no distiction between the more obvious gifts, such as preaching and teaching, and the less visible ones, like healing and listening. All are equal in God's sight. Being filled with the Spirit isn't an excuse for self-indulgence – it's the basic driving force for the whole of our Christian life and ministry.

Chapter Five

LOOK ALIVE

It's usually pretty obvious when things are alive. In winter a plant can seem to be dead, just a brown stick in the ground. Yet if you look closely the buds are there, admittedly very tiny, that'll open out in the spring into full leaf. Under the soil, out of sight, the root system is developing so that in summer a beautiful plant will once again burst into a cascade of colour. And all around it the weeds start to spring up, too! A baby before birth will kick its arms and legs and its mother knows from the little bumps that her child is alive. Finally it emerges into the light of day and she knows it's alive not just by the kicking but by the noise as well. Things that are alive move, react to their environment, grow and develop.

The same is true of the Christian life – spiritual life is as clear as any other kind. We'll grow and develop spiritually, react to our world in a Christian way, and so on. Those around us, be they work colleagues, friends or family, should be able to tell that we are Christians. There's a lovely poster showing a little monk standing in a courtroom, obviously on trial. The caption reads, 'If you were on trial for your faith, would there be enough evidence to convict you?' Let's take a look at some of the areas where that evidence might be seen.

Relationships

There are few things more fraught in the whole of human existence than how we get on with other people. Conflict is close to the heart of our human nature. The happiest of families have an occasional flare-up, the most devoted of lovers have the odd tiff and neighbours don't always see eye-to-eye. More seriously, rival groups of football hooligans spoil for a fight and nations go to war over territorial disputes. Most great novels are great because of the success with which they draw out and underline the complexities of human relationships and the disasters that can follow when they break down and fall apart.

Becoming a Christian isn't going to solve all your problems with other people straight away. There'll be conflicts and strife until the end of time. But it does start to make a difference – in you! You won't see everyone with rose-coloured spectacles, or develop a convenient blindness to everyone's faults. As you're filled with the same quality of love that Jesus showed, you'll start to become more compassionate and caring; more willing to listen than to shout; more willing to understand than to criticise negatively; more ready to put other people's interests ahead of your own. Paul said in his letter to the Philippians: 'Your attitude should be the same as that of Christ Jesus, who being in very nature God, did not consider equality with God something to be grasped, but made himself nothing, taking the very nature of a servant, being found in human likeness' (Philippians 2:5-7).

The Church has plenty of detractors, who are very ready to point out all its faults, but appear to be blind to the good it's done. Of course it hasn't been perfect, and we shouldn't pretend otherwise. But it's astonishing how often Christians have had a positive effect on relationships and people-issues. Lord Wilberforce campaigned for the abolition of slavery against much opposition to start with. St Francis led the way in his generation in caring for the poor and looking after God's creation. In our own century, Mother Theresa has shown almost unparalleled concern and love for the homeless of Calcutta; so has Jackie Pullinger for the triad members and drug addicts of Hong Kong. They're all ordinary Christian men and women who have achieved great things for God's Kingdom because they were open to his leading and filled with the Holy Spirit – not super-saints, but Christians like us.

Of all the signs of spiritual life in a Christian, none has a greater impact than the way relationships can be transformed. Indeed, when those who profess Christianity peddle feelings of hatred and violence and division, we start to wonder about how genuine their faith is. Someone once said that God doesn't ask us to like everyone – but he does call us to love them. That's infinitely more demanding and only possible because of the love of Jesus within us. Anyone can start among family and friends – who knows where it might end?

At work

It's all very well being a Christian in church – everyone expects it there. They'll be pleased you're thinking of Confirmation and will be delighted that you want to express your faith this way. They'll support you when you stand up for what you believe in. It's a different matter at work. Most of your colleagues are unlikely to be bothered about your personal beliefs, until you challenge them. Then they might well get upset if you find some of their practices unacceptable. What they consider to be a 'perk' you may feel is dishonesty; racial prejudice and sexual harassment are things you may feel you have to condemn openly. Putting a bit extra on the expenses, being 'economical with the truth' – in these and other areas of working life, you may well find that you're swimming against the tide. It certainly won't make you popular. But there's no need to spend all your time being negative. However little influence you think you've got, you'll be surprised at what you can achieve in God's strength. Perhaps someone's being victimised or treated unfairly – could you set an example by not joining in, and going out of your way to get alongside that person? If you're unhappy about the atmosphere, why not talk to someone in authority about changing the policy? If you're at a senior level yourself why not set the example in building fair and equitable working relationships in the workplace. Would you do without some of your perks, so that someone else could be paid more? Most issues are nothing like as cut and dried as that, but openness and integrity count for a lot, especially when they're in short supply as recent scandals have shown. Make sure that at work you're honest and straightforward in all you do, whatever your level of authority. You spend a lot more time at work than at church – that's one place where you'll be *seen* living the Christian life.

Opinions

We all love to air our views, on every subject from cabbages to kings. Politics, the economy, the environment, health . . . there's plenty for us to talk about. We're bound to form opinions, especially on subjects that affect us directly. Unfortunately those opinions are often based on inaccurate information, and coloured by our own prejudices. Becoming a Christian doesn't give all our opinions a factual basis, nor does it mean that we're automatically right. But our worship, our daily prayer and meditation and our relationship with God should have some effect on our opinions. We won't always agree with other people – even with other Christians. There are politicians on both sides of Parliament who hold very different views on how the country should be run, but who still join together as Christians to share and express their common faith. The Holy Spirit won't supply us with simple answers to all the intractable problems of our world, but if he fills our hearts and minds certain things will follow:

- We'll be a bit more willing to listen to those we disagree with and more considerate in how we express our different views.

- We'll be less inclined to jump to hasty and ill-founded conclusions, based on prejudice and passion. Instead we'll try to listen to all sides of a case, and think carefully before taking sides.

- We'll be less judgemental of those who don't see things our way.

- Our opinions should lead to action. It's all well and good to discuss the plight of the homeless or the handicapped – but we need to do what we can in their interests as well.

Evangelism

This is a word many people will shy away from. It smacks of well-heeled American preachers persuading gullible viewers to part with their money, or persistent and unwelcome callers at the front door. Evangelism isn't a sub-department of the Church's activities, run by the real enthusiasts and designed to bring in new members and increase funds. It's a way of life to which all Christians are called – getting new recruits is at best a secondary aim. The primary aim is to bring other people into a living relationship with God through Jesus Christ, so that they can experience God's love and grace as we have. As often as not we proclaim the good news about Jesus by the way we live and behave; the fact that we live the Christian life may well cause them to ask us questions about it, but nobody will come to faith in Christ through clever talking.

Haranguing is one way not to win converts! Those who respond to that sort of pressure are probably doing so from fear or guilt rather than because they've experienced the new life which Jesus offers. The mere fact that your faith is on view, that your colours are nailed to the mast, speaks volumes to others. That in itself may provoke them to ask you more about your faith and give you the opportunity to answer the questions which trouble them most.

Proclaiming the Christian faith isn't a sales pitch. You should be courteous and open in all your conversations, as willing to listen as to talk. But there are times when it's right to discuss Christianity openly; you don't need to be ashamed of what you believe in. If you aren't convinced yourself of the validity of your faith, it's not likely that you'll convince anyone else.

Facing opposition

In the Western World there's little direct opposition to Christianity. Religious tolerance is the order of the day. Compared to the recent experience of churches in the

Soviet bloc or in some Third World countries, those in the West have virtually no real experience of suffering or state antagonism. No one's been beaten up or arrested for their Christian beliefs, nor are parents forbidden to teach their children about the Christian faith. But there are other more subtle kinds of opposition – ridicule, isolation, rejection or even anger. We shouldn't be too surprised at this. Jesus himself aroused a great deal of controversy and hostility – so much so, that eventually he was killed as a criminal. Just before his arrest he said to his disciples, 'If the world hates you, keep in mind that it hated me first' (John 15:18). As followers of Jesus and members of God's Kingdom, we can expect such reactions from time to time. People will find our views and attitudes slightly quaint by comparison with theirs – we may be written off as naive and credulous. Going to church regularly may well exclude us from other regular Sunday activities, such as sport or clubs, that may give some folk the idea that we're not interested in them. At times we could find ourselves arousing considerable anger when we make a stand. Things might be said about us which are unkind or untruthful, or our reputations might be smeared. Peter wrote in his first letter to persecuted Christians of the first century, that if we walk with Christ and enjoy new life in him, we can 'greatly rejoice, though now for a little while you may have had to suffer grief in all kinds of trials' (1 Peter 1:6).

We can't experience anything that Jesus hasn't been through before us, and his Holy Spirit will give us all the courage and strength we need to cope with it, come through it and carry on serving God.

In Chapter 5 of his letter to the Galatians, Paul tells them that their lives as Christians must bear 'the fruit of the Spirit'. Confirmation is about receiving the Holy Spirit, as we've already seen. Paul wants his readers to know what sort of evidence they should look for that this had happened. He isn't telling us we have to be perfect, but that our lives will be radically different. In all our dealings with other people they should be able to see a contrast with what they usually see. At home and at work, when things are going well or when the problems are mounting up, the fruit of the Spirit will be in evidence. No Christian can expect to be exempt from sadness, anxiety or opposition – Jesus had to endure all of them. The difference is in the way they affect us and how we face up to them.

All these areas and others too will put our faith on trial. The Christian life is a battle – as the newly-baptised are reminded when the congregation encourages them to 'continue his faithful soldier and servant to the end of your life'. Paul even wrote in his letter to the church at Ephesus that we need spiritual armour from God to help us in that battle (Ephesians 6:10-20). Anyone who thinks that being a Christian is an easy option is sadly mistaken. However, there's no need to be discouraged or back off – Jesus said to his disciples, 'Take heart! I have overcome the world.' (John 16:33). Jesus came to the world to defeat once and for all the forces of evil. As those who share his risen life we also share in that victory. When you're confirmed you announce that you're going to follow in his ways, knowing what the consequences of that might be; you also know that the Holy Spirit who lives in you, will equip you to face them.

Chapter Six

THE LIFE-SUPPORT SYSTEM

Confirmation is about belonging, both to God and to his family, the Church. We can't be Christians in isolation – we need the community and fellowship of other believers for help, support and encouragement. At the same time, we have to learn to 'stand on our own two feet' in the Christian life. An astronaut who walks in space or on the moon couldn't do so without a vast range of back-up assistance both on earth and in his spacecraft. But once he's out there he depends entirely for his survival on his life-support system.

Personal prayer and Bible study as a daily habit is the heartbeat of our faith, our 'life-support' system. We don't have to wait until the next church service or fellowship group meeting to renew our relationship with God. Daily prayer is our direct access to God. He's with us all the time by his Holy Spirit and we can approach him whenever we want to have a conversation with him. We don't have to feel cut off.

Reading the Bible

It may seem rather strange to suggest reading each day from a book whose most recent pages were written all but two thousand years ago. There are many great works of literature, philosophy and science which are undisputed masterpieces, but no one suggests they're read for private devotions. What's so special about the Bible?

We've seen how God's creation reveals to us a great deal about his character and mind. But Christians have always believed that the Bible teaches us even more about God and his purposes. The picture it gives is far more detailed than creation. In the Bible we see God in action throughout the history of his people Israel and on a far deeper level we recognise how God speaks to us, relates with us and guides us, even 2,000 years later. Daily Bible-reading has always been a part of the Church's tradition and heritage, and the Church of England, in common with most other churches, has a 'lectionary' to ensure that we read the Bible thoroughly each year and don't just concentrate on our favourite parts.

The Bible is a kind of library. It isn't just one book but sixty-six separate ones, written over a period of a thousand years or more. Some people have read it from cover to cover, but it's not always an easy book to read or understand and for most of us the best approach is to study certain parts. As a starter, if you aren't familiar with the Bible, why not buy an inexpensive basic guide to the different books of the Bible, its themes and characters? You might also find it helpful to use daily Bible reading notes, such as those produced by Scripture Union, the Bible Reading Fellowship, or *Every Day with Jesus*. These aren't meant to be the last word in scholarship but will get you into a habit of daily Bible reading and show you ways of letting it speak to you. Not all of the Bible makes sense at first. You may feel that some of the Old Testament is rather obscure in meaning or that Paul's letters don't always speak deeply to you. But at other times you'll discover that the words leap off the page at you, suddenly making sense of what's happening in your life. Then again, you may also find that the Bible makes you feel uncomfortable, or challenges you to take a particular course of action. Don't be put off by some of the common misconceptions about the Bible. It shouldn't be dismissed as fairy-tales, nor is it a product of a past age that has no significance for the twentieth century. Approach it with an open mind and heart, allow the Holy Spirit to reveal its meaning for you and you'll discover there's no end to its riches.

There would be many good reasons for reading the Bible as literature, quite apart from the Christian faith. But as Christians we don't read it primarily for historical information or moral guidance. It's God's Word to us, and in its pages we hear his voice speaking to us. Through it we see more of his will for us and for the world. In Jesus we recognise not just a great moral teacher, but also someone utterly unique, whose integrity bore out his claims about his relationship with his heavenly Father.

It's in God's written word that we come into contact with the Living Word, Jesus himself (see John 1).

We may not always feel like reading from the Bible each day – and there'll be times when we struggle to work out what it means for us, when it seems to make little sense, or makes us feel uncomfortable. That's why a habit of daily prayer is so important. God is worthy of our worship and praise all the time, not just when we feel like it. As part of our daily worship, reading the Bible is enriching and eye-opening, provided that we persevere and open our hearts to what God is saying to us. Even if we don't understand everything, often a phrase or idea will stay in our hearts throughout the day, or even longer, to deepen our love for God and strengthen us in our faith.

Talking to God – and listening

Good relationships are founded on good communications. If we fail to write letters to our friends or phone them up, the friendship will soon come to grief. A husband and wife who don't talk to each other are probably well on their way to a marital breakdown! In our conversations we communicate to others our thoughts and feelings and learn more about them. The more we communicate with someone else, the better we get to know them. That leads to greater trust and confidence in the relationship, especially in a time of crisis.

Our relationship with God works in the same way. Its depth depends on how much we talk to him and listen to what he tells us. He doesn't just want to hear from us when things go wrong, but equally when we want to thank him, to worship him, to find out his will. He understands how we feel and never turns us away even if we don't much feel like coming to him.

All great Christians have made a habit of prayer each day. Martin Luther used to tell people that he had so much to do that he couldn't possibly do it all unless he prayed first for three hours! John Wesley was also noted for the time he spent in prayer. Sometimes we'll find praying difficult, at other times it'll be a joy. There aren't any fixed rules about how to do it, because it isn't a technique – it's a relationship.

- *Prayer is focusing on God.* When we look through a camera viewfinder our eye is drawn to the subject; we then focus on it until we can see it clearly. God is the centre of our focus and attention – as we look at him we forget about ourselves and we can concentrate on his glory and power, his love and mercy, his majesty and his forgiveness. So much of our misery is caused by spending too much time thinking about ourselves. Once we fix our eyes on God and get him into perspective, we begin to see ourselves more clearly: after all, he made us in his own image and likeness.

- *Prayer is entering God's will.* There's no chance that we will ever 'bend God's ear' or negotiate with him to see things our way! Prayer isn't for the closed mind, that comes to God having decided already what he ought to do. Prayer is opening our minds and wills to God, allowing him to change our attitudes so that we see things as he sees them. We won't always be certain of God's will, and at times we'll struggle to stay on his path as other events threaten to push us off balance. God doesn't necessarily show us the whole of our journey with him, but he will give us all we need to cope with the stage we've reached. As we pray for people and situations, we are sometimes conscious that God is speaking to us, helping us to pray in accordance with his will. Paul wrote to the church at Rome, 'We do not know what we ought to pray, but the Spirit himself intercedes for us' (Romans 8:26). God knows and hears our prayers even before we've prayed them and his Spirit within us draws us ever more closely to him.

- *Prayer is committing ourselves to God.* By focusing on God and entering into his will we're committing ourselves to his ways, whatever that may cost. God dislikes nothing more than apathy and lack of commitment. Prayer is hard work – in one sense very simple, but also extremely demanding of our time and energy.

It may require of us not just faith, but action too. It's a very good thing to pray for poor old Miss Jones who's housebound and lonely, but part of the answer to our prayer for her may be that we ought to pay her a visit occasionally. If our prayers and faith don't have some tangible results (however inadequate we may feel they are), we stand open to being accused of hypocrisy by those who aren't Christians. In praying for the world we pray for our part in it too, insignificant though that may seem. As we ask God to bless, heal, renew or transform, we ask him to do that afresh to us and acknowledge our part in his plan for what we're praying.

- *Prayer is being renewed each day.* Renewal isn't something that only happens when we become a Christian. It's true that a basic and vital change takes place then, but our Christian life is a constant process of being changed. As we turn to God in prayer, we open ourselves to his love and power, to the Holy Spirit giving us fresh guidance and new spiritual vitality. The psalmist wrote, 'In my distress I called to the Lord; I cried to my God for help. From his temple he heard my voice . . . He reached down from on high and took hold of me.' (Psalm 18:6, 16). It's often as we cry out to God in a moment of great need that we discover his power to 'reach down and take hold of us', to transform our despair into hope, and fill us with the joy of the Holy Spirit. As we experience his unconditional and unlimited love when we come into his presence so we're renewed and grow more to be like him. It's a slow process and we make many mistakes on the way, but when we look back on our walk with God, we realise how far he's brought us.

- *Prayer is believing God will act.* There wouldn't be much point in praying to God if he never did anything. He'd either be powerless or callous! We bring our concerns to God in faith, believing that he'll act on our requests. That doesn't mean whatever we ask for – if our prayers are all self-centred we need first to learn to see things God's way. God answers prayer as he knows is best, even if we don't understand why things haven't worked out as we thought they should. God asks us to trust him and leave the results of our prayer in his powerful and loving hands. We don't usually like relinquishing control, but doing so is a vital part of our prayer life.

- *Prayer is enjoying God's presence.* God wants us to enjoy his presence. We may find it hard to believe, but the most important element in our prayers is relaxing with God, listening to him, and rejoicing in his love and grace. He's our loving Father and wants us to come to him. The Prodigal Son arrived home to a party in his honour undeserving though he was; that's how it should be when we come to God.

Ideas for approaching prayer

Be yourself – God knows us inside out (Psalm 139:1-4). Papering over the cracks is no use because he sees us as we are. There's no point in pretending to be what we're not, because he accepts us with all our faults and failings, and understands our feelings and pressure-points. In his presence we can be fully ourselves.

Be quiet – It's impossible to listen properly when we're still talking. We should take time to be silent with God, to meditate on his word, to hear his voice. We live in a noisy and confusing world and we need to experience God's peace in order to see things clearly again.

Be open – If we hold on to our prejudices and wrong attitudes, we shut out the power of the Holy Spirit to change us. God wants us to enter his will, to be guided by him.

Be simple – God doesn't demand a theology degree or lots

of long words. He doesn't score our prayers on their length or complexity. When Jesus taught his disciples the pattern for all prayer, he didn't use long, learned expressions – the Lord's Prayer isn't wordy or involved. We can pray using whatever words come naturally to us and as the Holy Spirit leads us.

Be imaginative – Why get stuck with words at all? It's just as good to picture the situation we're praying for in our mind's eye. If a picture occurs to us as we pray, we can let our minds dwell on it or develop it.

Be thankful – Paul told the Philippians, 'In everything, by prayer and petition with thanksgiving, make your requests known to God' (Philippians 4:6). Gratitude to God should be the recurring theme of every prayer; God has given us so much to rejoice in and be thankful for. Remembering to thank God also prevents too much complaining!

There'll be times when your prayers don't seem to work and just bounce back off the ceiling. God isn't keeping a tally of how many 'good' prayer times you have, and he knows when circumstances make it difficult to spend much time. But it's worth cultivating the habit of daily prayer and Bible study, because without it, the Bishop's prayer from Isaiah 11 in the Confirmation service can't be answered. God's Spirit comes upon us when we turn and open our hearts to him.

THE CONFIRMATION SERVICE

You may well be wondering why Confirmation is necessary at all. Nowhere is it mentioned in the Bible and the Early Church didn't practise it in the way we do. Baptism, by contrast, is spoken of frequently in the New Testament, and appears in some ways to be the more important rite. It may therefore seem odd that any priest may administer Baptism, but only a Bishop can confirm.

Approaching Confirmation

In the Early Church you became a Christian and were baptised almost at the same time, you would then receive the Holy Spirit by the laying on of hands. Only later did these events become widely separated in time. High infant mortality rates meant that people wanted their children baptised as soon as possible. Bishops were taking responsibility for larger and larger areas (called dioceses), and rarely could they be present at a Baptism to lay their hands on the person concerned. This happened much later on. After the Reformation, the Church of England in effect turned Confirmation into a rite for teenagers to enable them to ratify the faith their parents and godparents had professed on their behalf at baptism. Beforehand, the candidates had to learn the basis of the Christian faith (the Catechism) which then formed part of the service.

The Alternative Service Book returns us to something like the practice of the Early Church by providing a service which includes Baptism, Confirmation and a Eucharist, presided over by a Bishop. Those who come to faith in adulthood are baptised and confirmed at the same time and immediately become full members of the Church and able to receive the bread and wine. Not all Confirmations take place in such a service, and many are confirmed who were baptised as infants, so it's quite possible for Confirmation to have a service to itself, without Baptism or the Eucharist. If you've not yet been baptised, that must happen before you're confirmed and should be performed by the Bishop at the same service. The rite is exactly the same as for infants, except that parents and godparents aren't in evidence. If you were baptised as an infant, then you'll have to renew your baptismal promises, and this happens just before you're confirmed. Whatever the particular service in which your Confirmation takes place, the rite itself remains exactly the same.

Renewal of baptismal vows

The candidates stand before the Bishop; he says:

You have come here to be confirmed. You stand in the presence of God and his Church. With your own mouth and from your own heart you must declare your allegiance to Christ and your rejection of all that is evil. Therefore I ask these questions:

Do you turn to Christ?
Answer **I turn to Christ.**

Do you repent of your sins?
Answer **I repent of my sins.**

Do you renounce evil?
Answer **I renounce evil.**

Then the Bishop says:

You must now declare before God and his Church that you accept the Christian faith into which you were baptised and in which you will live and grow.

Do you believe and trust in God the Father, who made the world?
Answer **I believe and trust in him.**

Do you believe and trust in his Son Jesus Christ, who redeemed mankind?
Answer **I believe and trust in him.**

Do you believe and trust in his Holy Spirit, who gives life
to the people of God?
Answer   **I believe and trust in him.**

The Bishop turns to the congregation and says:

This is the faith of the Church.
All   **This is our faith**
          We believe and trust in one God,
          Father, Son and Holy Spirit.

The Confirmation

The Bishop stands before those to be confirmed and says:

Our help is in the name of the Lord
All   **Who has made heaven and earth.**

Blessed be the name of the Lord
All   **Now and forever. Amen.**

The Bishop stretches out his hands towards them and says:

Almighty and everliving God,
you have given your servants new birth
in baptism by water and the Spirit,
and have forgiven them all their sins.
Let your Holy Spirit rest upon them:
the Spirit of wisdom and understanding;
the Spirit of counsel and inward strength;
the Spirit of knowlege and true godliness;
and let their delight be in the fear of the Lord.
Amen.

The Bishop lays his hand on the head of each candidate, saying:

Confirm, O Lord, your servant N with your Holy Spirit.

and each one answers:

Amen.

*After confirmation, the Bishop invites the people to join with him
and say:*

Defend, O Lord, your servants with your
heavenly grace,
that they may continue yours for ever,
and daily increase in your Holy Spirit more and more,
until they come to your everlasting kingdom.
Amen.

There are four elements to Confirmation

1 The baptismal vows are confirmed by the candidates
This is primarily for those who were baptised as infants and
who are now making those promises for themselves. Those
who've been baptised just previously may feel as though
they're in for a 500-mile service! However, it reinforces the
importance both of becoming a Christian and of believing
in the Christian faith. Confirmation is inextricably linked
with Baptism and the inclusion of the promises at this
point is intended to emphasise that connection.

2 The Confirmation Prayer is said by the Bishop
Before he does, however, he announces to the congregation
that 'Our help is in the name of the Lord', to which they reply,
'who has made heaven and earth'. The responses at this
point are more than just a warning that the Confirmation
itself is about to start. It also serves to focus our attention
away from what's happening onto God, through whom
alone it's possible.

The Prayer itself is very ancient and is based very closely
on Isaiah 11. It hasn't been altered much over the centuries,
and is a prayer specifically for the candidates, who will
normally be standing or kneeling in front of the Bishop by
this stage. Its words stress again the fact that new birth and
forgiveness are the basis of becoming a Christian, and the
importance of Baptism in this. From now on, the candidates
are going to live the Christian life publicly, and they'll only
do this in the power of God's Holy Spirit, whom the Bishop
asks God to send upon them. He prays for three aspects of
receiving the Spirit and living in his strength:

- *Understanding.* We all have to continue to grow in our understanding of Christianity, not just as an intellectual exercise, but much more as a way of helping us to grow as Christians and recognise how our faith contributes to our everyday life.

- *Strength.* We need God's help day-by-day to face all the challenges and difficulties of being a Christian in a sometimes hostile environment.

- *Spirituality.* We grow more and more to be like Jesus as we seek God's will and try to serve him. God doesn't just want us to do things for him. He wants us to take time to enjoy his presence – to pray and meditate and to live more and more in a way which pleases him.

We won't always succeed – in fact we'll fail far more often than we'd want – but as we look back we'll be able to see how far God has brought us and how he's helped us.

3 *The Bishop then lays hands on each candidate*
The candidate kneels in front of him, asking that the Holy Spirit will confirm each one. This is the Confirmation itself. It sets the seal on all that God has done for each individual up to this point, and as they're confirmed with the Holy Spirit, so they're in a sense being 'sent out' to live the Christian life.

4 *The congregation joins the Bishop in praying for the candidates.*
The prayer stresses the forward-looking element of Confirmation, requesting God to defend those who've been confirmed and keep them in himself, and help them to grow daily in his Spirit until they come to be with him for ever. If the Eucharist is to follow, the Peace will be shared at this point, a practical sign that the candidates will be received at the Lord's Table.

The significance of the service

What does Confirmation actually mean? There are all sorts of views on this question, but most of them would fit under one of the following descriptions:

- It expresses the candidate's Christian commitment. Those who are confirmed are making a clear stand for the beliefs of Christianity and publicly affirming their own turning to Christ, repentance for their sins and rejection of evil. It certainly won't be the only time they want to announce this – there are other occasions in life which bring about this desire. But it's an important occasion nonetheless and often the first time they'll have been so public about their faith.

- It is an occasion when the Holy Spirit is received in a very conscious way. The Confirmation Prayer brings this out and highlights why the Spirit is a vital part of our walk with God. Again, there are other times when they'll be especially aware of the Holy Spirit coming upon their lives, but this may well be the first.

- Confirmation provides a connection both with Baptism and the Eucharist, and the provision of a service which includes all three brings us more into line with the practice of the Early Church.

- It looks to the future and to the life which those confirmed will now live in the strength of the Holy Spirit. The candidates are being sent out to be Christians in the world.

- It ratifies that the candidates belong to God's Church and particularly to the branch of it called the Church of England.

It is usually understood that confirmation presupposes both that you've prepared properly for the commitment you're going to express and that you'll continue afterwards to live as a Christian, particularly to participate in the worship of the Church and receive Communion. In one way Confirmation may feel like an end in itself, but it's only the end of one stage of your journey.

A QUESTION OF FAITH

The most influential and effective Christians are generally the most thoughtful ones. Christian activity which isn't grounded in personal prayer, meditation and thinking through the faith, is usually rather superficial. The following questions aren't meant to be a test to see how well you've done so far, instead they're designed to get you thinking about what you believe as a Christian and what that implies for your daily life. There aren't any right answers. While you could answer them on your own and for yourself, you'll probably find it very helpful to discuss the issues raised with whoever's preparing you for Confirmation. Alternatively, you might like to discuss them with other candidates, or those who've recently been confirmed. In any event, don't try to avoid them – they're too important to ignore!

1 What significance has your Baptism had for you? If you've not been baptised yet, what effect do you think it'll have on you? Does Baptism make you a Christian, and if not, what's its significance?

2 Did you become a Christian in a clear-cut decision at one point in time, or was it a gradual process? What difference does it make to you now that you are a Christian? What does it mean to you to be 'born again'?

3 Are traditional Christian beliefs, as expressed in the Creed, at all relevant in the twentieth century? Why does it matter what we believe about God, Jesus and the Holy Spirit?

4 Christians have long argued over what they believe, in their attempt to find the truth. At what point do such disputes become damaging? Is it possible to define exactly what Christian belief is and where should the line be drawn between truth and error?

5 How important is it for you to receive the bread and

wine regularly? How do you understand the Eucharist, and what does it do for you?

6 What for you is the primary reason for being confirmed?

7 What gifts has the Holy Spirit given you to enable you to serve God both in the Church and in the world? How do you think you'll be able to use them?

8 What's the most important part of worship for you? Do you think this is true for most of the other Christians you know?

9 You probably prefer a particular style of worship – try to think about why you respond to it and why some other ways of worshipping may leave you feeling cold.

10 What do you think will be the biggest challenges and difficulties of being a Christian in your workplace, family, neighbourhood, circle of friends, etc?

11 What problems have you found, or might you find, in establishing a pattern of daily prayer and Bible study?

12 How do you think you can grow in your prayer life? Do you find any particular approaches or styles of praying helpful?

TAKE THE PLUNGE

Before he can jump out of an aircraft safely, a parachutist has to be properly trained and equipped. He must know how his parachute works and how to operate it correctly; he needs to learn how to land without breaking a leg; he must find out where he's supposed to land so that he jumps out at the right time; he may also work out the height and speed of the aircraft. All this is interesting but rather academic – unless he actually gets to the point where he leaps out into space and pulls the ripcord! He needs to take the plunge. The same is true of a diver – however much he knows about the theory of diving and however much he may train in the gym to get his body fit, if he doesn't leap into the water it will all be useless.

It's important that you're properly prepared for being confirmed – it isn't something to undertake lightly and you should have a basic idea of the Christian faith. You may learn a great deal about the Bible and the Church; you may have all sorts of gifts and abilities, but if you don't use them they won't be useful. Like the parachutist or the diver, you have to take the plunge and live the Christian life for real! You don't need a divinity degree to be a Christian and you don't have to undergo special training – Christianity isn't just for specialists!

It may be that you've already made a decision to be confirmed, but it is also possible you are still undecided. Inevitably, there are certain pressures on you to say 'yes' or 'no'. At the end of the day only *you* can make that decision. Your local church will be delighted, your family may also be very pleased (though that won't be true for everyone), and you might have friends who will be pleased if you're confirmed with them. Other people will probably try to deter you. All these things will affect you, but the decision is yours alone. There are always reasons for putting it off – you can never be quite sure what you're letting yourself in for, or what other people may think of you. But you aren't doing it for your family, or even for the Church. You're making this public statement about your faith in God through Jesus Christ to demonstrate your commitment to his ways and determination to live in a way which pleases him. It's him you're following. He loved you enough to send his Son to this earth to live and die for you. He accepts you just as you are and offers you his forgiveness and love, without any conditions at all. He's promised you his Holy Spirit to guide you and help you every day and give not just the strength you need to serve God but a lot more besides! Your commitment to him is your expression of your love for him, and when you declare it publicly, as you do at Confirmation, you're telling the rest of the world that you think he's worth every ounce of it.

After you've read this book, perhaps there will be Confirmation to follow – if there is, you'll discover for yourself that it's both an end and a beginning. It's the end of stage one of your Christian life, but the start of a whole new life in the power of the Spirit. That won't be easy. You'll have plenty of hurdles to jump, and there will be times when you'll feel like giving up. The Christian life never stops, however. God knows how we feel and he's given us his Spirit to guide, strengthen and inspire us. There are many decisions to take after Confirmation, many more points of commitment and recommitment, and many more times when you'll have to take the plunge. If you trust God to hold on to you, he'll never let you go – his hands will always keep you. If there is Confirmation to follow, you can be certain that there's a whole new life to follow Confirmation.